Baby Bear's
hiding place

Story by Beverley Randell
Illustrations by Isabel Lowe

2

One day, Father Bear said,
"I'm going into the forest
to find some food.
You can come with me,
Baby Bear."

"Oh, good," said Baby Bear.
"I will get my basket."

Baby Bear went into the forest with Father Bear.

"Look at all the red berries in my basket!" said Baby Bear.

"You are a good little bear," said Father Bear.

Then Baby Bear
saw a big tree.
"I can climb this tree,"
he said, and up he went.

"I'm going to climb
all the way to the top,"
said Baby Bear.

But then Baby Bear
saw a big hole
in the tree.
"I can get
inside this hole,"
he said.

Baby Bear went into the hole.
He looked down.

"I can see Father Bear,"
he said,
"but he can't see me.
I can **hide** from him in here."

Father Bear said,

"Come on, Baby Bear.

We are going home, now.

Where are you?"

"I can see Baby Bear's basket,
but I **can't** see him,"
said Father Bear.
"Is he lost in the forest?"

"Boo!" said Baby Bear.

"I'm hiding up here

in my little tree house!"